BE YOUR OWN MAN

by Jessica Sanders
Art by Robbie Cathro

FIVE MILE

For Ben Schlaer,

A wonderful man who had the most kind and
generous heart.

J.S.

Made with love by the team at

FiVE M.LE

Michelle, Rocco, Jacqui, Graham, Claire, Sarah, Bridget, Kate & Tillie

Five Mile,
the publishing division
of Regency Media
www.fivemile.com.au

First published 2020
This paperback edition published 2023

Written by Jessica Sanders
Text copyright © Jessica Sanders, 2020
Visit: www.re-shape.info

Jessica Sanders asserts her right to be identified as the author of this work.

Illustrations by Robbie Cathro
Illustration copyright © Robbie Cathro, 2020

Robbie Cathro asserts his right to be identified as the illustrator of this work.

Author photo on page 39 by Katja Kollecker

Printed in China 5 4 3 2 1

A catalogue record for this
book is available from the
National Library of Australia

Note to the reader

For the boys,

It is my hope that this book will support you
to love and care for all the parts of you.

I want you to celebrate what makes you
different, because that's what makes you, you.

And I want you to explore and express
your emotions. Because when you do,
anything is possible.

So, dream big.

Your friend,
Jess

Author's note

This book has been written for boys and those who identify as a boy.
The messages within were informed by my postgraduate studies in gender
and social work as well as my experiences working with youth. It's my hope
that this book will encourage boys and men to embrace their vulnerability
and to be their authentic selves. A world where everyone feels free to be
themselves is a safer and better world for all.

Be Your Own Man has been created to be understood by a range of readers.
Children younger than the recommended reading age of 8+ should be able
to navigate the book with the support of a parent, carer or teacher.
Even if a child is not able to understand all of the language, they should
understand the visual messages.

There is absolutely no-one else quite like you,
and that's amazing!

Every boy is different.

But does it sometimes feel like there is just one way to be a boy?

act a certain way,

Have you ever felt you should ...

wear certain clothes,

or do certain activities

... just because you're a boy?

If you do find yourself ever feeling this way,
it's really important that you know this ...

Boys don't have to be tough.

Boys don't have to be sporty.

Boys don't even have to be funny.

All a boy has to be is himself.

So what kind of boy are you?

Are you a boy who uses his voice to stand up for others?

Or a boy who loves to sing, dance and play music?

Are you a boy who loves to move his body and be part of a team?

Or perhaps you are a boy who listens carefully to what others have to say and offers the world's best hugs!

Maybe you are a boy who does all these things and more...

It's important to love and accept all the parts of you. What really matters is that you do your very best and don't compare yourself to others. We are all different and we all have different strengths and abilities.

Your friends should bring out the best in you and celebrate all the parts of you.

Good friends are kind and respect who you are and what you need. Spending time with people who make you feel safe to be yourself is an important part of being your own boy.

You and your body are together for life, so always
treat your body like you would your own best friend.

When you are your own best friend, you love yourself for what is on the inside and the outside.

This kind of love is called 'self-love'.

You can practise self-love ...

- by speaking to yourself like you would your own best friend.

- by asking for help when you need it.

- by writing down all the things that you love about yourself, and that make you, you.

- by giving yourself a big hug and whispering, "Thank you, body, for all that you do for me".

Your body is your home. It will take you on exciting adventures and allow you to experience all the wonderful things this world has to offer.

There is no such thing as the perfect body.
Every body is unique and every body is a
good body.

Your body is seriously smart! It can speak to you by sending signals. Your body will tell you when you need to eat and when you need rest. It's important to listen to your body's signals and give your body what it needs.

Your body will also let you know when things are not quite right. You might get a racing heart, sweaty palms or even start to shake.

You might also hear your own voice inside your head telling you something is not quite right. If you ever feel this way, listen to your body and let a grown-up know what has happened straightaway.

Our emotions are formed in our brain, but we can actually feel them in our bodies. That's why they are called feelings!

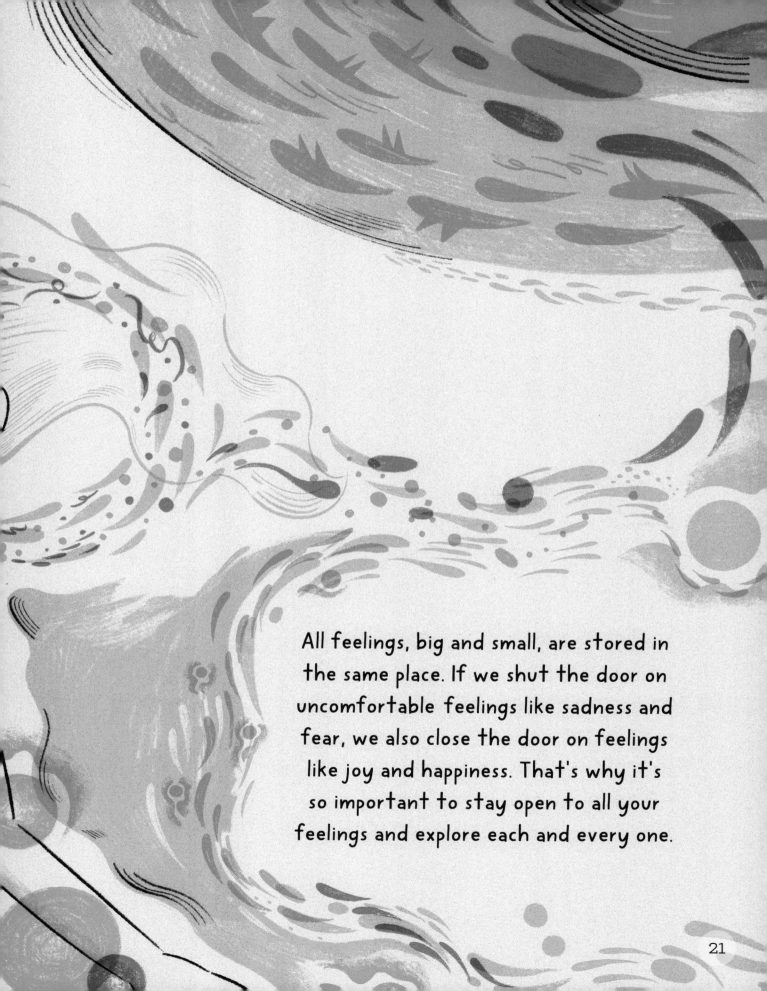

All feelings, big and small, are stored in the same place. If we shut the door on uncomfortable feelings like sadness and fear, we also close the door on feelings like joy and happiness. That's why it's so important to stay open to all your feelings and explore each and every one.

When we ignore our feelings
they don't just disappear. They become
trapped inside of us, with nowhere to go. They begin to
grow bigger and weigh us down. It can become difficult
to carry around these heavy feelings each day.

But when we explore our emotions and feelings by expressing them, we are able to let them go. This leaves us feeling lighter and more free!

We all express and release our emotions in different ways, so it's important to find activities that work for you.

Here are some activities you could try!
Different feelings usually need
different activities, so pick one that
suits how you are feeling and give it a go.
Another word for these activities is 'self-care'.
Self-care is a skill you will use throughout your
whole life. It's an important part of being
healthy and happy.

If you're feeling angry ...

Move your body!
You could climb a tree, jump
on a trampoline, go for a
walk or run, even shoot a
basketball.

Find a quiet spot and close
your eyes. Try to count your
breaths as you breathe in and
out. Do this until you feel your
mind and body relaxing.

Put on your favourite tunes
REALLY LOUD and dance crazily
just for you! It feels great to
be a bit silly sometimes.

Talk about how you are feeling
with someone you trust.
Speaking our feelings out loud
helps us to understand them.

Draw your feelings! What
would they look like on paper?

If you're feeling sad ...

Help a friend or family member. It can be a relief to get out of your own head and help others. Plus, it feels really good to do something nice for someone else.

Write your feelings down in a special journal. You'll feel a lot better when your thoughts are out of your head and written down on paper.

Tell yourself you are doing okay and that nothing lasts forever — our feelings are always changing, and this sad feeling will also pass.

Ask somebody you love for a hug.

Have a big cry and let out all your tears.

If you're feeling worried ...

Put on some comfy clothes and find a quiet spot to read a book or watch TV.

Spend some time in nature. Find a shady tree or lovely patch of grass, and take in all that you can see.

Learn how to knit, crochet, cross stitch or draw mandalas. It's really calming to concentrate on one thing and use your hands.

If you're feeling low, angry or just overwhelmed and
nothing is helping you feel better, it's important to reach
out to a trusted adult or one of the organisations listed
on pages 34 and 35 of this book.

Everyone has to ask for help sometimes, even grown-ups.
It's an important skill to learn. It might feel a bit scary
at first, but once you do ask for help you will feel
like a big weight has been lifted from you.

When you put up your hand and ask for help,
it encourages others to do the same.

And when you share your feelings with your friends,
you are letting them know that they can share their
feelings too. This is really powerful!

So remember ... you can be the kind of boy who helps others to feel free to be themselves.

You can be a boy who is brave enough to share both the highs and the lows.

Someone who is strong enough to be himself and show others what is in his heart.

A boy who is kind enough to celebrate the differences between himself and others.

Someone who stands up for change and supports those around him.

You can be anything.

You can be everything.

All you need to do is to be your own boy,
so that you can become your own man.

The kind of person
you were always
meant to be.

Always reach out for support

If something came up for you when you were reading this book, it's important to share those feelings with an adult you trust. This could be your teacher, a parent or carer, or your coach.

If you don't want to talk to someone you trust, or if you feel as though you don't have that special someone, there are people who would love to support you. Here are some places you can turn to for help and support.

Australia

Kids Helpline — 1800 551 800
Contact Kids Helpline at any time, for any reason.
Online chat: https://kidshelpline.com.au

Butterfly Foundation National Helpline — 1800 334 673
Support for eating disorders and body image concerns.
Online chat: www.thebutterflyfoundation.org.au

Headspace — 1800 650 890
Support for young people and their families going through a tough time.
Online chat: https://eheadspace.org.au/

New Zealand

What's Up — 0800 942 8787
A safe place to talk about anything at all.
Online chat: www.whatsup.co.nz

Youth Line — 0800 376 633
Support for young people and their families.
Online chat: www.youthline.co.nz

More about gender

'Boy' or 'girl' are labels that are commonly used to talk about children. But they aren't the right fit for everyone. Here are some awesome books that don't use labels at all.

On a magical do-nothing day by Beatrice Alemagna

Who am I? I am me! by Jayneen Sanders

Neither by Airlie Anderson

If you're in Australia and feeling a bit confused about gender in general, you can call Qlife, who know all about it! If you're in NZ, you can call What's Up or Youth Line.

Qlife — 1800 184 527
Open 3pm until midnight
Online chat: www.qlife.org.au

Let's talk ... discussion questions

Have you ever felt that you had to change part of yourself to fit in? Why do you think you felt like that? Do you think you've ever made someone feel like they had to change a part of themselves to fit in? How do you think we can all create a world where everyone feels safe to be themselves?

After reading this book, what do you think being your own man means?

CELEBRATE YOUR STRENGTHS

What does it mean to celebrate your strengths?

Remember that strengths aren't just physical. For example, one of your strengths could be kindness.

What are some of your strengths?

Your body helps you eat, play and hug. Why are you grateful for your body?

What kind of feelings do you think this boy has been ignoring? Why do you think he ignored those feelings?

What are some of the ways that you express and release your feelings?

Who would you ask for help if you needed it? Why would you choose that person?

Why do you think it's important to use your voice to help others?

All available at www.reshape.info

Educator resources

Free lesson plans

Free student workbook

Book recommendations

Links to external resources

Parent and carer resources

Book recommendations

Top tips

Links to external resources

Jessica Sanders

Jessica is an author, advocate and social worker from Melbourne, Australia. Growing up, Jess always felt different and found it hard to fit in. There were times when she tried to act like the girls she saw in movies or magazines, but it never felt quite right. One day, Jess decided that she was never going to try to be anyone other than herself. This decision changed the course of her life. She was able to find friends who loved her just the way she was. And she began a journey that led her to become a social worker and then an author, whose mission it is to make every young person remember that they are wonderful, exactly as they are.

Robbie Cathro

Robbie is an illustrator and storyteller from Bristol, UK, who loves to create colourful, fun and thoughtful imagery for children's publications. Robbie loves picture books and animation for their extraordinary, magical takes on life, and how they can whisk you away into a new and exciting world. With his work he aims to replicate this feeling and combine it with positive messages, whether it's for a fantastical story or a grounded project that he can add a charm to. He wants to bring inclusive projects and resources into the world that weren't available for him growing up — books that allow kids to feel seen and that let them know they exist. Ultimately, he wants to provide a safe space where, when the reader closes the book, they feel reassured within themselves.